Sermon title: Date:

Notes:

Words I heard in the sermon today

God	☐	Faith	☐
Jesus	☐	Believe	☐
Holy spirit	☐	Bible	☐
Worship	☐	World	☐
Forgive	☐	Father	☐
Disciples	☐	Son	☐
Church	☐	Amen	☐
Pray	☐	Grace	☐
Joy	☐	Sin	☐
Love	☐	Saved	☐

Questions I have:

Prayers for others

Today's scripture passages:

Two ways I can use the lesson in my life:

How I feel...

Prayer for myself

My favorite song today

What I learned today

What I did not understand

Sermon sketches

Bible Story Comic Strip

Sermon title:

Date:

Notes:

Words I heard in the sermon today

God	☐	Faith	☐
Jesus	☐	Believe	☐
Holy spirit	☐	Bible	☐
Worship	☐	World	☐
Forgive	☐	Father	☐
Disciples	☐	Son	☐
Church	☐	Amen	☐
Pray	☐	Grace	☐
Joy	☐	Sin	☐
Love	☐	Saved	☐

Questions I have:

Prayers for others

Today's scripture passages:

Two ways I can use the lesson in my life:

How I feel...

Prayer for myself

My favorite song today

What I learned today

What I did not understand

Sermon sketches

Bible Story Comic Strip

Sermon title:

Date:

Notes:

Words I heard in the sermon today

God	☐	Faith	☐
Jesus	☐	Believe	☐
Holy spirit	☐	Bible	☐
Worship	☐	World	☐
Forgive	☐	Father	☐
Disciples	☐	Son	☐
Church	☐	Amen	☐
Pray	☐	Grace	☐
Joy	☐	Sin	☐
Love	☐	Saved	☐

Questions I have:

Prayers for others

Today's scripture passages:

Two ways I can use the lesson in my life:

How I feel...

Prayer for myself

My favorite song today

What I learned today

What I did not understand

Sermon sketches

Bible Story Comic Strip

Sermon title: **Date:**

Notes:

Words I heard in the sermon today

God ☐   Faith ☐
Jesus ☐   Believe ☐
Holy spirit ☐   Bible ☐
Worship ☐   World ☐
Forgive ☐   Father ☐
Disciples ☐   Son ☐
Church ☐   Amen ☐
Pray ☐   Grace ☐
Joy ☐   Sin ☐
Love ☐   Saved ☐

Questions I have:

Prayers for others

Today's scripture passages:

Two ways I can use the lesson in my life:

How I feel...

Prayer for myself

My favorite song today

What I learned today

What I did not understand

Sermon sketches

Bible Story Comic Strip

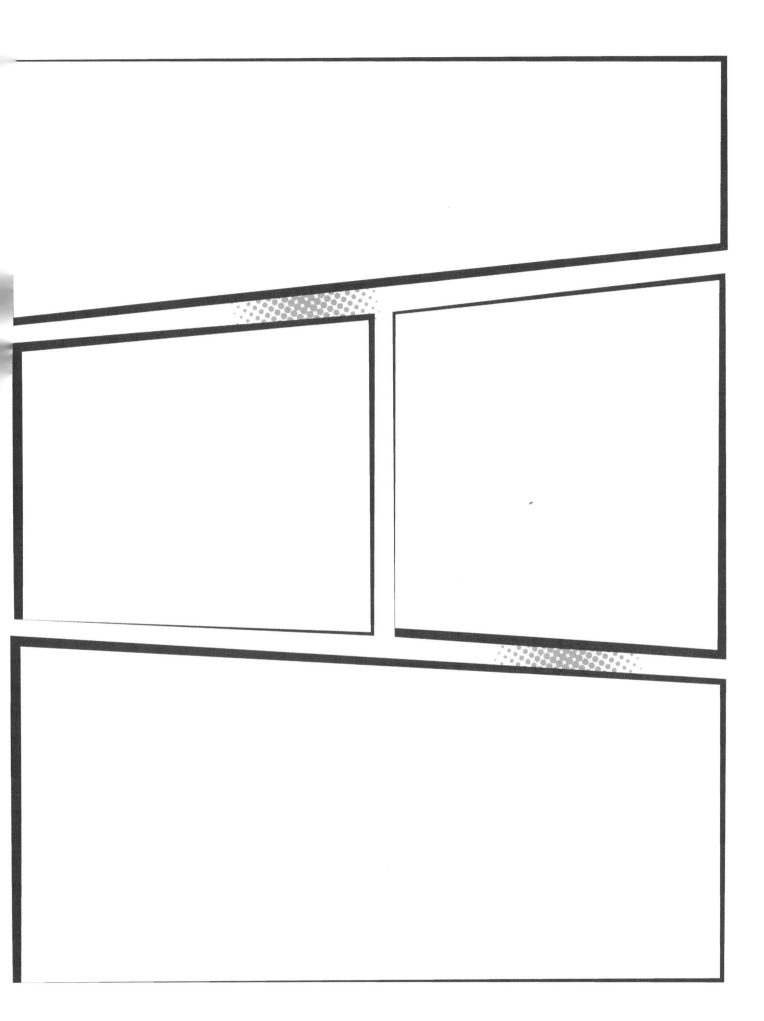

Sermon title: **Date:**

Notes:

Words I heard in the sermon today

God	☐	Faith	☐
Jesus	☐	Believe	☐
Holy spirit	☐	Bible	☐
Worship	☐	World	☐
Forgive	☐	Father	☐
Disciples	☐	Son	☐
Church	☐	Amen	☐
Pray	☐	Grace	☐
Joy	☐	Sin	☐
Love	☐	Saved	☐

Questions I have:

Prayers for others

Today's scripture passages:

Two ways I can use the lesson in my life:

How I feel...

Prayer for myself

My favorite song today

What I learned today

What I did not understand

Sermon sketches

Bible Story Comic Strip

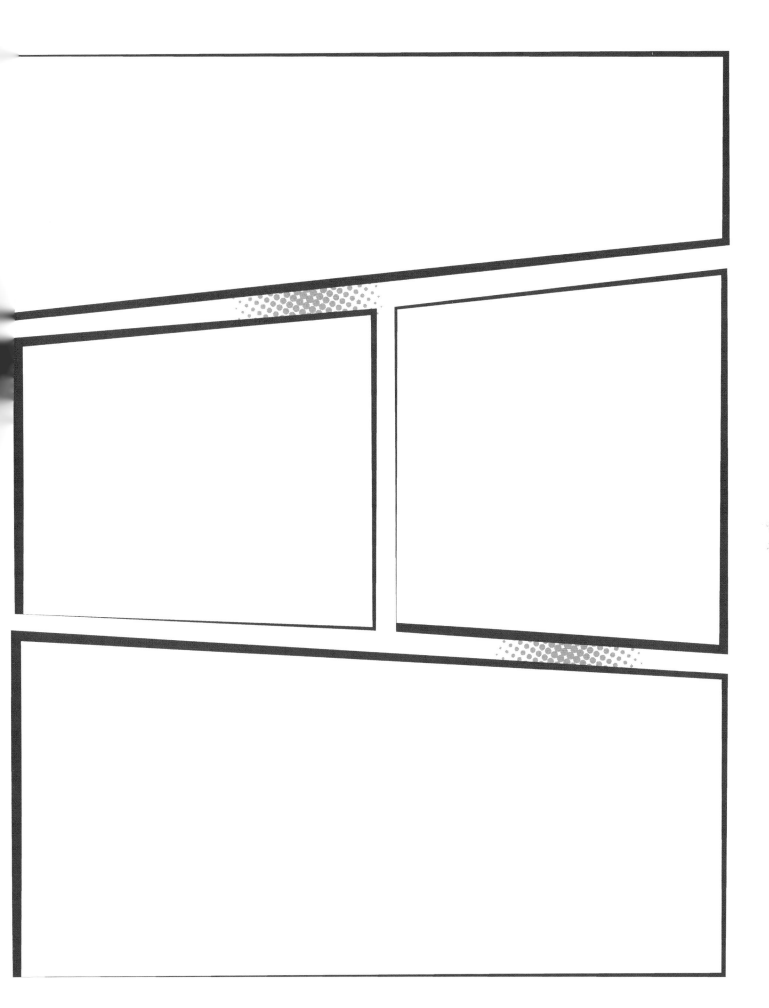

Sermon title:

Date:

Notes:

Words I heard in the sermon today

God	☐	Faith	☐
Jesus	☐	Believe	☐
Holy spirit	☐	Bible	☐
Worship	☐	World	☐
Forgive	☐	Father	☐
Disciples	☐	Son	☐
Church	☐	Amen	☐
Pray	☐	Grace	☐
Joy	☐	Sin	☐
Love	☐	Saved	☐

Questions I have:

Prayers for others

Today's scripture passages:

Two ways I can use the lesson in my life:

How I feel...

Prayer for myself

My favorite song today

What I learned today

What I did not understand

Sermon sketches

Bible Story Comic Strip

Sermon title: Date:

Notes:

Words I heard in the sermon today

God ☐   Faith ☐
Jesus ☐   Believe ☐
Holy spirit ☐   Bible ☐
Worship ☐   World ☐
Forgive ☐   Father ☐
Disciples ☐   Son ☐
Church ☐   Amen ☐
Pray ☐   Grace ☐
Joy ☐   Sin ☐
Love ☐   Saved ☐

Questions I have:

Prayers for others

Today's scripture passages:

Two ways I can use the lesson in my life:

How I feel...

Prayer for myself

My favorite song today

What I learned today

What I did not understand

Sermon sketches

Bible Story Comic Strip

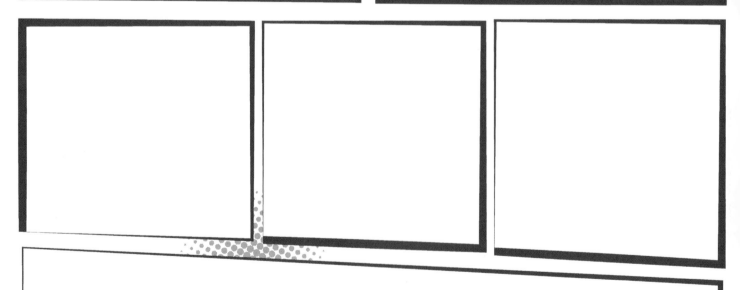

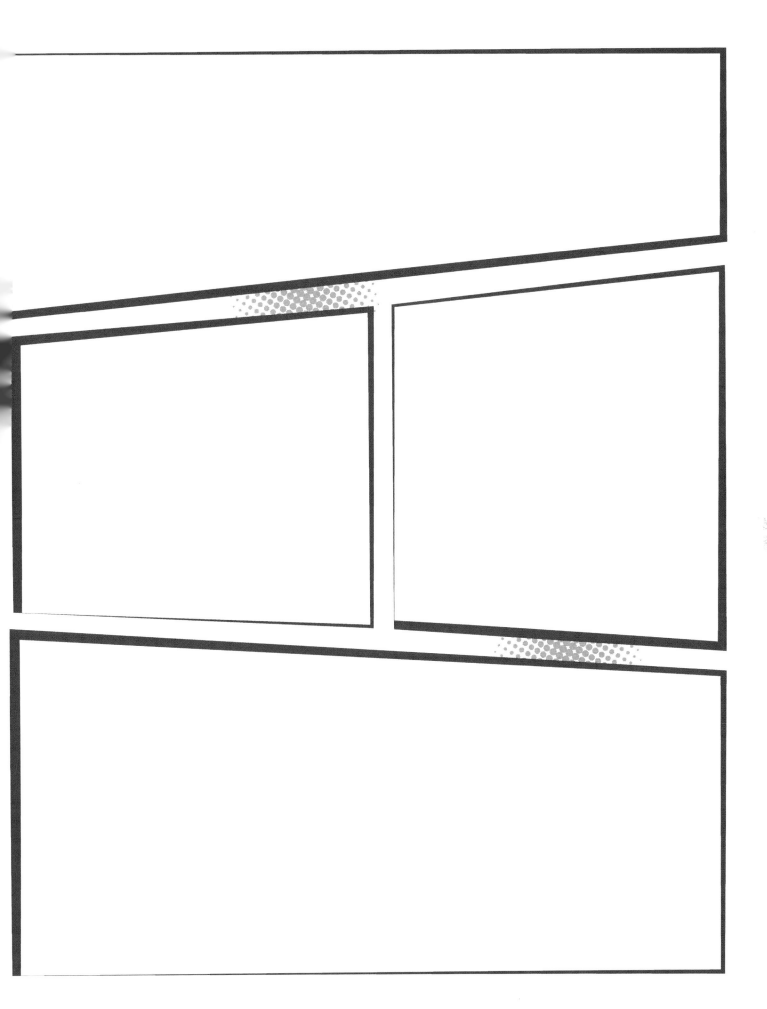

Sermon title: **Date:**

Notes:

Words I heard in the sermon today

God	☐	Faith	☐
Jesus	☐	Believe	☐
Holy spirit	☐	Bible	☐
Worship	☐	World	☐
Forgive	☐	Father	☐
Disciples	☐	Son	☐
Church	☐	Amen	☐
Pray	☐	Grace	☐
Joy	☐	Sin	☐
Love	☐	Saved	☐

Questions I have:

Prayers for others

Today's scripture passages:

Two ways I can use the lesson in my life:

How I feel...

Prayer for myself

My favorite song today

What I learned today

What I did not understand

Sermon sketches

Bible Story Comic Strip

Sermon title: Date:

Notes:

Words I heard in the sermon today

God   ☐   Faith   ☐
Jesus   ☐   Believe   ☐
Holy spirit ☐   Bible   ☐
Worship   ☐   World   ☐
Forgive   ☐   Father   ☐
Disciples   ☐   Son   ☐
Church   ☐   Amen   ☐
Pray   ☐   Grace   ☐
Joy   ☐   Sin   ☐
Love   ☐   Saved   ☐

Questions I have:

Prayers for others

Today's scripture passages:

Two ways I can use the lesson in my life:

How I feel...

Prayer for myself

My favorite song today

What I learned today

What I did not understand

Sermon sketches

Bible Story Comic Strip

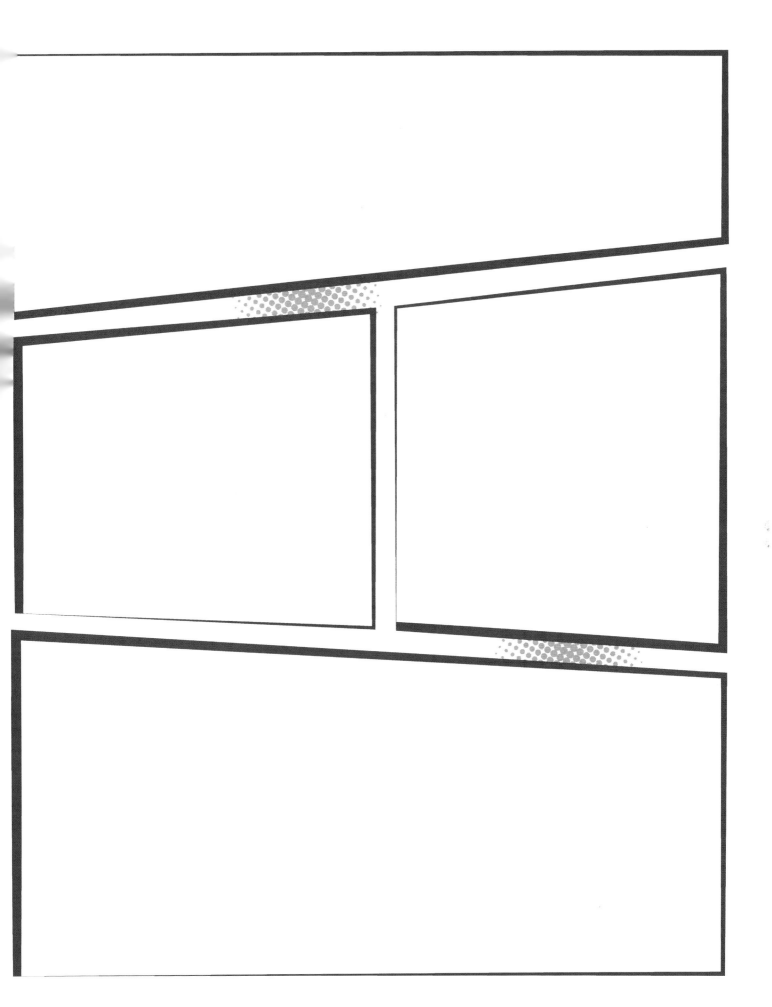

Sermon title: Date:

Notes:

Words I heard in the sermon today

God	☐	Faith	☐
Jesus	☐	Believe	☐
Holy spirit	☐	Bible	☐
Worship	☐	World	☐
Forgive	☐	Father	☐
Disciples	☐	Son	☐
Church	☐	Amen	☐
Pray	☐	Grace	☐
Joy	☐	Sin	☐
Love	☐	Saved	☐

Questions I have:

Prayers for others

Today's scripture passages:

Two ways I can use the lesson in my life:

How I feel...

Prayer for myself

My favorite song today

What I learned today

What I did not understand

Sermon sketches

Bible Story Comic Strip

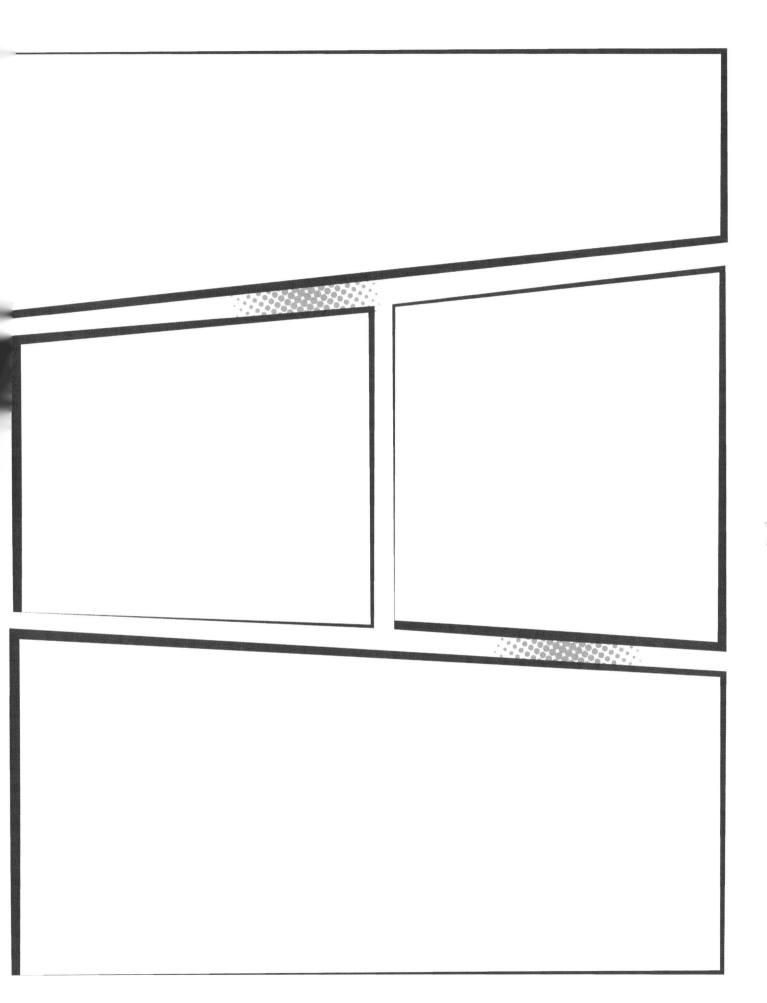

Sermon title:

Date:

Notes:

Words I heard in the sermon today

God	☐	Faith	☐
Jesus	☐	Believe	☐
Holy spirit	☐	Bible	☐
Worship	☐	World	☐
Forgive	☐	Father	☐
Disciples	☐	Son	☐
Church	☐	Amen	☐
Pray	☐	Grace	☐
Joy	☐	Sin	☐
Love	☐	Saved	☐

Questions I have:

Prayers for others

Today's scripture passages:

Two ways I can use the lesson in my life:

How I feel...

Prayer for myself

My favorite song today

What I learned today

What I did not understand

Sermon sketches

Bible Story Comic Strip

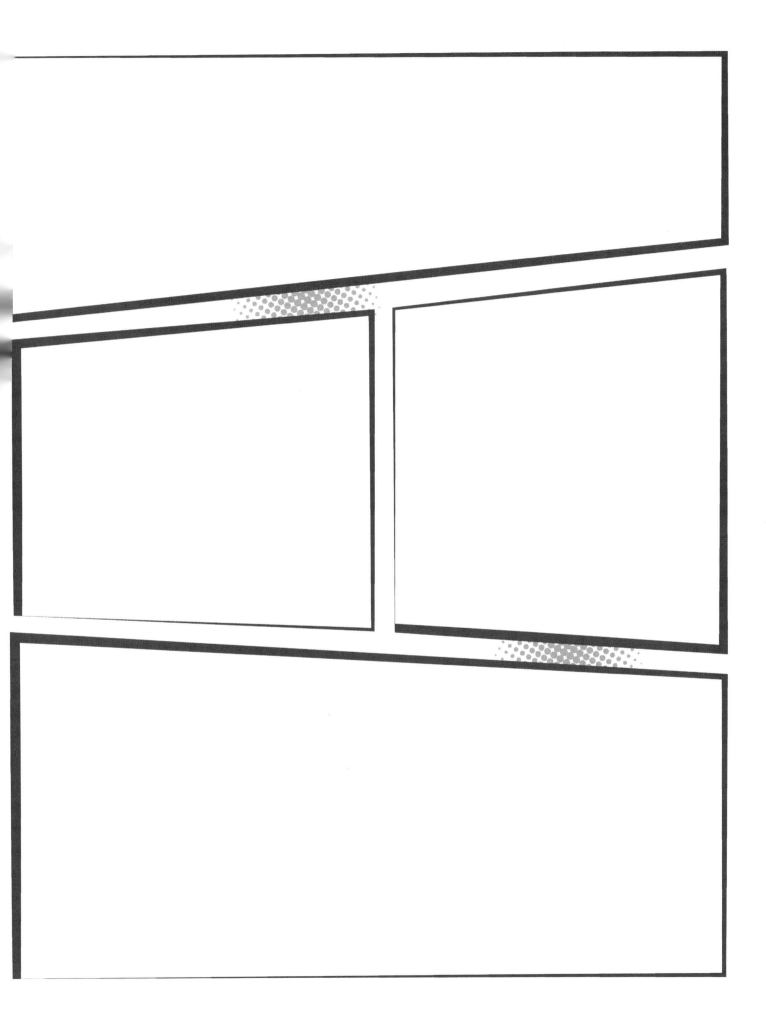

Sermon title: Date:

Notes:

Words I heard in the sermon today

God	☐	Faith	☐
Jesus	☐	Believe	☐
Holy spirit	☐	Bible	☐
Worship	☐	World	☐
Forgive	☐	Father	☐
Disciples	☐	Son	☐
Church	☐	Amen	☐
Pray	☐	Grace	☐
Joy	☐	Sin	☐
Love	☐	Saved	☐

Questions I have:

Prayers for others

Today's scripture passages:

Two ways I can use the lesson in my life:

How I feel...

Prayer for myself

My favorite song today

What I learned today

What I did not understand

Sermon sketches

Bible Story Comic Strip

Sermon title: Date:

Notes:

Words I heard in the sermon today

God	☐	Faith	☐
Jesus	☐	Believe	☐
Holy spirit	☐	Bible	☐
Worship	☐	World	☐
Forgive	☐	Father	☐
Disciples	☐	Son	☐
Church	☐	Amen	☐
Pray	☐	Grace	☐
Joy	☐	Sin	☐
Love	☐	Saved	☐

Questions I have:

Prayers for others

Today's scripture passages:

Two ways I can use the lesson in my life:

How I feel...

Prayer for myself

My favorite song today

What I learned today

What I did not understand

Sermon sketches

Bible Story Comic Strip

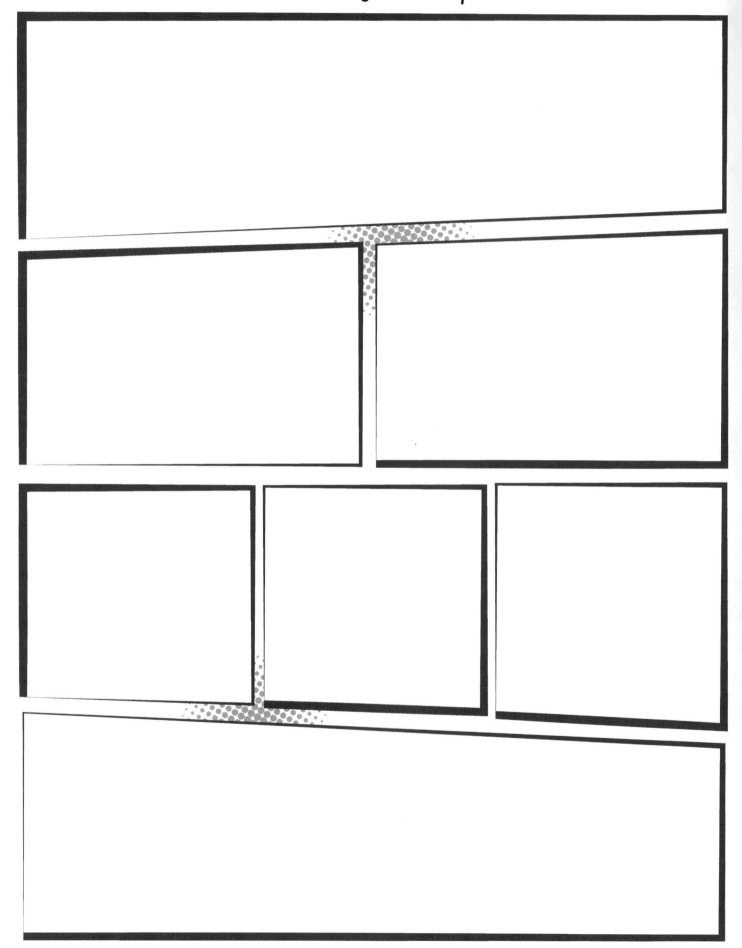

Sermon title: **Date:**

Notes:

Words I heard in the sermon today

God	☐	Faith	☐
Jesus	☐	Believe	☐
Holy spirit	☐	Bible	☐
Worship	☐	World	☐
Forgive	☐	Father	☐
Disciples	☐	Son	☐
Church	☐	Amen	☐
Pray	☐	Grace	☐
Joy	☐	Sin	☐
Love	☐	Saved	☐

Questions I have:

Prayers for others

Today's scripture passages:

Two ways I can use the lesson in my life:

How I feel...

Prayer for myself

My favorite song today

What I learned today

What I did not understand

Sermon sketches

Bible Story Comic Strip

Sermon title:

Date:

Notes:

Words I heard in the sermon today

God	☐	Faith	☐
Jesus	☐	Believe	☐
Holy spirit	☐	Bible	☐
Worship	☐	World	☐
Forgive	☐	Father	☐
Disciples	☐	Son	☐
Church	☐	Amen	☐
Pray	☐	Grace	☐
Joy	☐	Sin	☐
Love	☐	Saved	☐

Questions I have:

Prayers for others

Today's scripture passages:

Two ways I can use the lesson in my life:

How I feel...

Prayer for myself

My favorite song today

What I learned today

What I did not understand

Sermon sketches

Bible Story Comic Strip

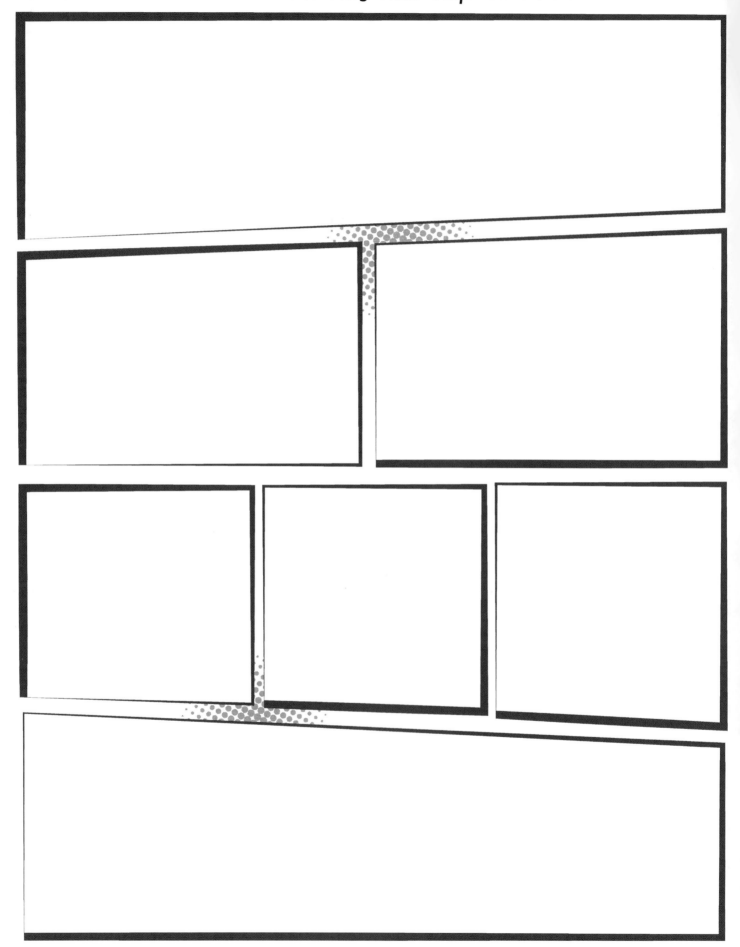

Sermon title:

Date:

Notes:

Words I heard in the sermon today

God ☐   Faith ☐
Jesus ☐   Believe ☐
Holy spirit ☐ Bible ☐
Worship ☐   World ☐
Forgive ☐   Father ☐
Disciples ☐   Son ☐
Church ☐   Amen ☐
Pray ☐   Grace ☐
Joy ☐   Sin ☐
Love ☐   Saved ☐

Questions I have:

Prayers for others

Today's scripture passages:

Two ways I can use the lesson in my life:

How I feel...

Prayer for myself

My favorite song today

What I learned today

What I did not understand

Sermon sketches

Bible Story Comic Strip

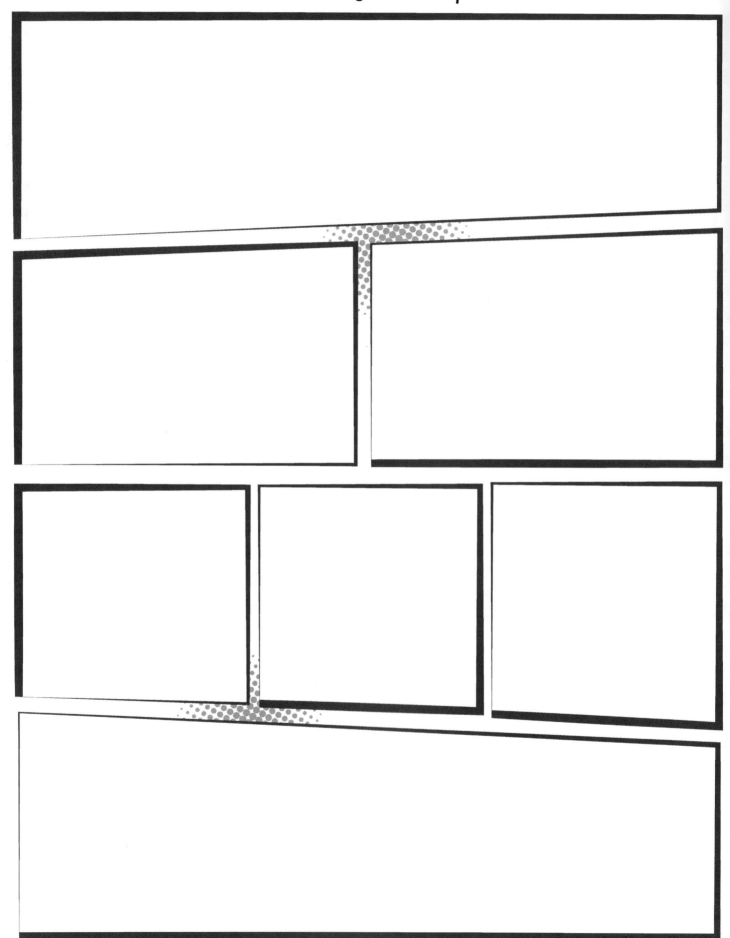

Sermon title: Date:

Notes:

Words I heard in the sermon today

God	☐	Faith	☐
Jesus	☐	Believe	☐
Holy spirit	☐	Bible	☐
Worship	☐	World	☐
Forgive	☐	Father	☐
Disciples	☐	Son	☐
Church	☐	Amen	☐
Pray	☐	Grace	☐
Joy	☐	Sin	☐
Love	☐	Saved	☐

Questions I have:

Prayers for others

Today's scripture passages:

Two ways I can use the lesson in my life:

How I feel...

Prayer for myself

My favorite song today

What I learned today

What I did not understand

Sermon sketches

Bible Story Comic Strip

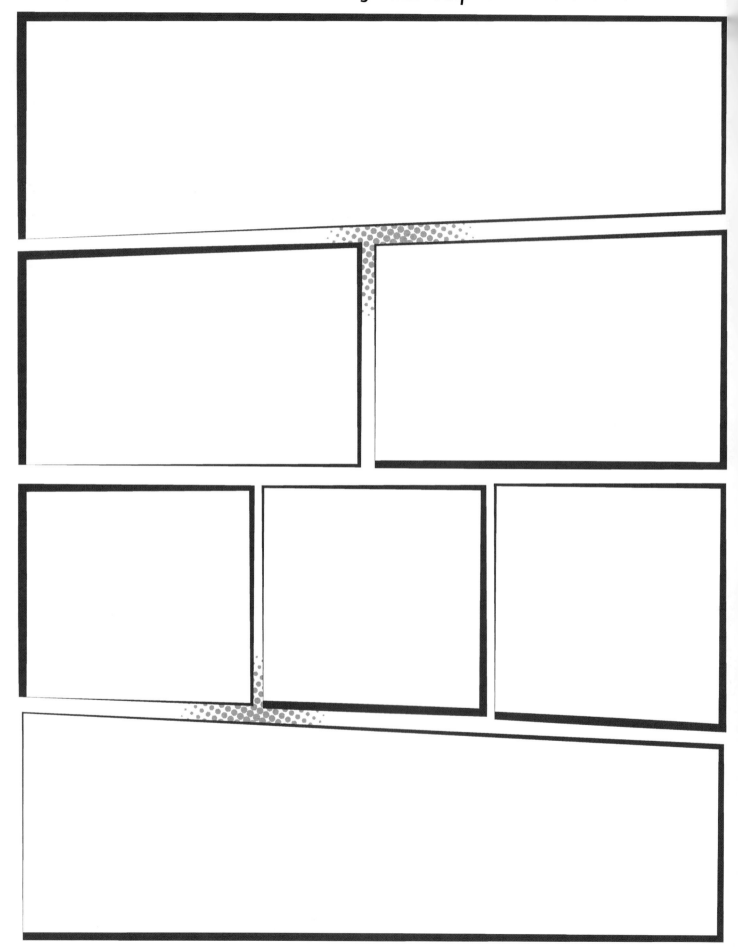

Sermon title: **Date:**

Notes:

Words I heard in the sermon today

God ☐	Faith ☐
Jesus ☐	Believe ☐
Holy spirit ☐	Bible ☐
Worship ☐	World ☐
Forgive ☐	Father ☐
Disciples ☐	Son ☐
Church ☐	Amen ☐
Pray ☐	Grace ☐
Joy ☐	Sin ☐
Love ☐	Saved ☐

Questions I have:

Prayers for others

Today's scripture passages:

Two ways I can use the lesson in my life:

How I feel...

Prayer for myself

My favorite song today

What I learned today

What I did not understand

Sermon sketches

Bible Story Comic Strip

Sermon title: Date:

Notes:

Words I heard in the sermon today

God	☐	Faith	☐
Jesus	☐	Believe	☐
Holy spirit	☐	Bible	☐
Worship	☐	World	☐
Forgive	☐	Father	☐
Disciples	☐	Son	☐
Church	☐	Amen	☐
Pray	☐	Grace	☐
Joy	☐	Sin	☐
Love	☐	Saved	☐

Questions I have:

Prayers for others

Today's scripture passages:

Two ways I can use the lesson in my life:

How I feel...

Prayer for myself

My favorite song today

What I learned today

What I did not understand

Sermon sketches

Bible Story Comic Strip

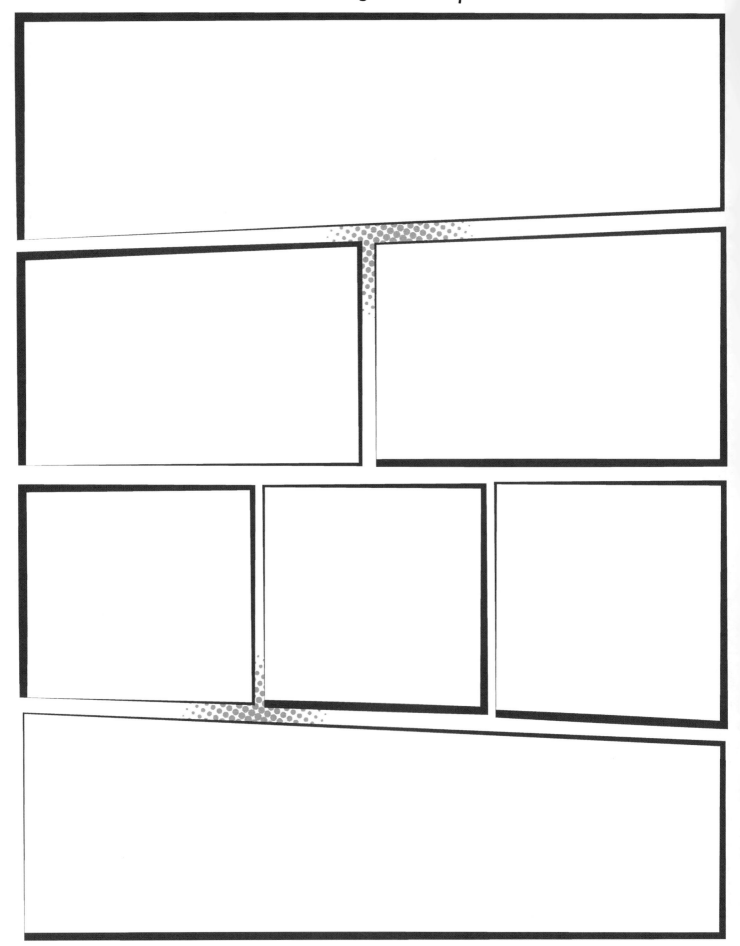

Sermon title: **Date:**

Notes:

Words I heard in the sermon today

God	☐	Faith	☐
Jesus	☐	Believe	☐
Holy spirit	☐	Bible	☐
Worship	☐	World	☐
Forgive	☐	Father	☐
Disciples	☐	Son	☐
Church	☐	Amen	☐
Pray	☐	Grace	☐
Joy	☐	Sin	☐
Love	☐	Saved	☐

Questions I have:

Prayers for others

Today's scripture passages:

Two ways I can use the lesson in my life:

How I feel...

Prayer for myself

My favorite song today

What I learned today

What I did not understand

Sermon sketches

Bible Story Comic Strip

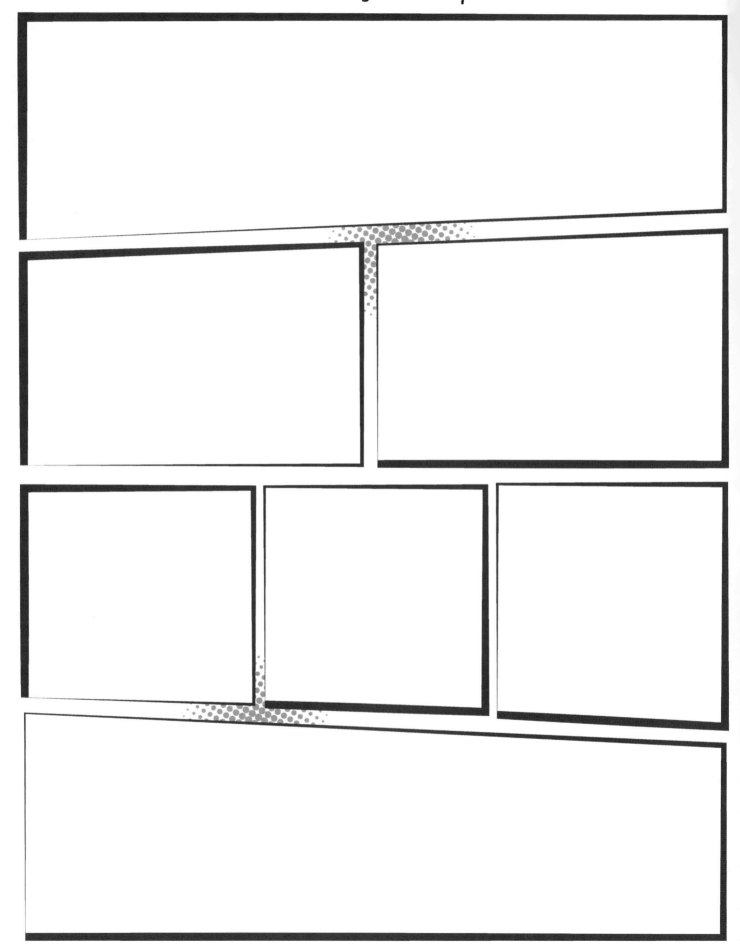

Sermon title: Date:

Notes:

Words I heard in the sermon today

God	☐	Faith	☐
Jesus	☐	Believe	☐
Holy spirit	☐	Bible	☐
Worship	☐	World	☐
Forgive	☐	Father	☐
Disciples	☐	Son	☐
Church	☐	Amen	☐
Pray	☐	Grace	☐
Joy	☐	Sin	☐
Love	☐	Saved	☐

Questions I have:

Prayers for others

Today's scripture passages:

Two ways I can use the lesson in my life:

How I feel...

Prayer for myself

My favorite song today

What I learned today

What I did not understand

Sermon sketches

Bible Story Comic Strip

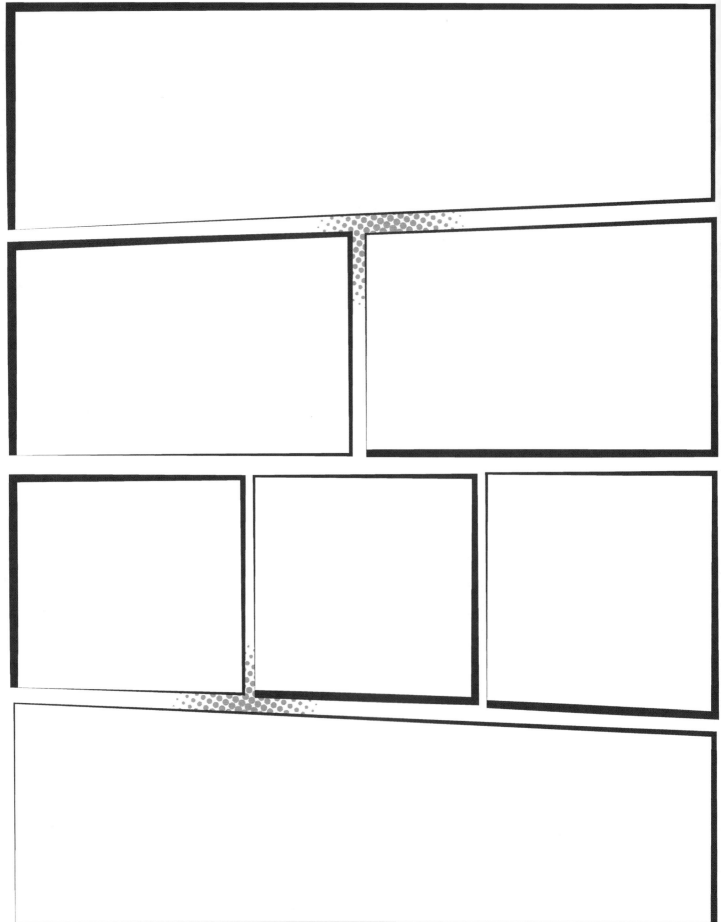

Sermon title: Date:

Notes:

Words I heard in the sermon today

God	☐	Faith	☐
Jesus	☐	Believe	☐
Holy spirit	☐	Bible	☐
Worship	☐	World	☐
Forgive	☐	Father	☐
Disciples	☐	Son	☐
Church	☐	Amen	☐
Pray	☐	Grace	☐
Joy	☐	Sin	☐
Love	☐	Saved	☐

Questions I have:

Prayers for others

Today's scripture passages:

Two ways I can use the lesson in my life:

How I feel...

Prayer for myself

My favorite song today

What I learned today

What I did not understand

Sermon sketches

Bible Story Comic Strip

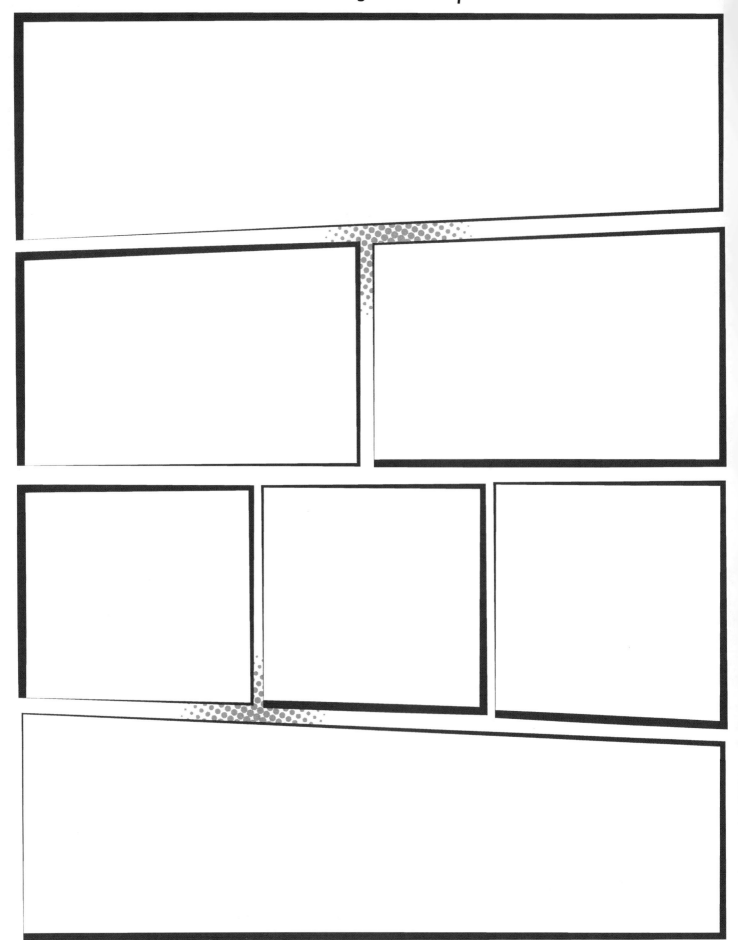

Sermon title:

Date:

Notes:

Words I heard in the sermon today

God	☐	Faith	☐
Jesus	☐	Believe	☐
Holy spirit	☐	Bible	☐
Worship	☐	World	☐
Forgive	☐	Father	☐
Disciples	☐	Son	☐
Church	☐	Amen	☐
Pray	☐	Grace	☐
Joy	☐	Sin	☐
Love	☐	Saved	☐

Questions I have:

Prayers for others

Today's scripture passages:

Two ways I can use the lesson in my life:

How I feel...

Prayer for myself

My favorite song today

What I learned today

What I did not understand

Sermon sketches

Bible Story Comic Strip

Sermon title: **Date:**

Notes:

Words I heard in the sermon today

God	☐	Faith	☐
Jesus	☐	Believe	☐
Holy spirit	☐	Bible	☐
Worship	☐	World	☐
Forgive	☐	Father	☐
Disciples	☐	Son	☐
Church	☐	Amen	☐
Pray	☐	Grace	☐
Joy	☐	Sin	☐
Love	☐	Saved	☐

Questions I have:

Prayers for others

Today's scripture passages:

Two ways I can use the lesson in my life:

How I feel...

Prayer for myself

My favorite song today

What I learned today

What I did not understand

Sermon sketches

Bible Story Comic Strip

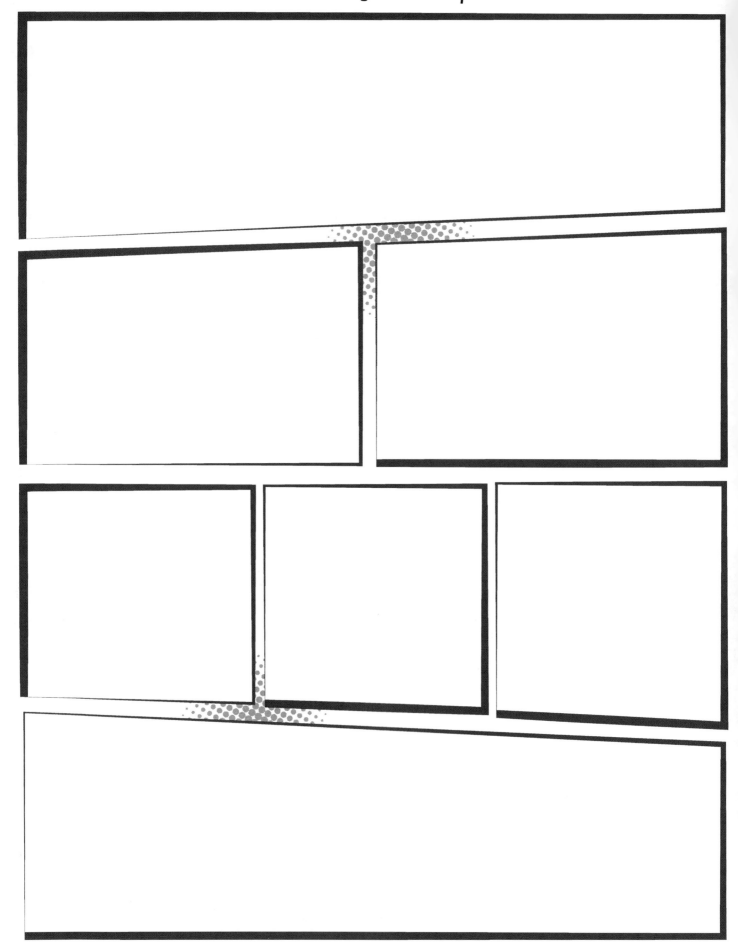

Made in the USA
Middletown, DE
28 May 2025

76220426R00055